Forex Trading Indicators

Best top 7 free high win rate indicators

Abraham Robert. C

TABLE OF CONTENT

CHAPTER 3

MOMENTUM INDICATORS

RELATIVE STRENGTH INDEX (RSI)

The Relative Strength Index: Things to Be Aware of

USING RSI AND OTHER INDICATORS IN TRADING

RSI with Moving Averages (MA)

RSI with Bollinger Bands

RSI with MACD

RSI with Stochastic Oscillator

CHAPTER 4

VOLATILITY INDICATORS

AVERAGE TRUE RANGE (ATR)

HOW TO TRADE USING ATR

Breakouts

The Signal Line Method

Size of Position

BEST ATR INDICATOR COMBINATIONS

The Parabolic SAR and ATR

ATR and Stochastics

BOLINGER BAND

Using Bollinger Bands to Trade

ADVANTAGES AND THE DISADVANTAGES OF BOLLINGER BANDS TECHNIQUES

CHAPTER 5

Chapter 1

Overview of Forex Indicators

Forex indicator is a computation in mathematics that lets you examine a pair of currencies. To assist you in understanding the movement in the currency, it may take into account volume, open interest, exchange rates, and other variables. Graphs, bars, and charts are often used to display this data so you can choose whether to proceed with a long or short position.

With this knowledge at hand, traders may make better-informed choices and perhaps increase their earnings.

A very important note; a chart with more indicators does not always indicate more information or better trading choices, despite the common misconception among novice traders that more is better. Many technical indicators are either duplicates or alternatives to more information.

Having an excessive amount of data on your chart that makes it difficult to understand does not provide any benefits.

Your efforts will be ineffective as hesitation might arise while choosing whether to carry out a market order.

Technical indicators are only instruments, and when used improperly, they may provide unreliable outcomes.

It is up to you to decipher the technical indicator you have plotted on your charts and produce a signal that will tell you when to join the market, when to raise stop losses, when to take a partial profit, and when to close a trade.

Plotted on the chart of the selected market, indicators may indicate future price reversals, the direction and intensity of price trends, and the momentum of price movements. The kind of indicator used such as a trend-following, momentum, volatility, or volume indicator determines what the indicator tracks.

Although indicators predict probable price movement based on analysis of pertinent market data, including price and trading volume, there is no assurance that the outcome will be as anticipated.

Because of this, a lot of traders choose to filter out inconsistencies by basing their conclusions on a mix of similarities across different indicators. Even so, it's crucial to effectively manage your risk and take into account other pertinent elements.

The Four Categories of Forex Indicators

The four primary types of technical indicators are trend volume, volatility, momentum.

Certain indicator are categorized into two categories, and it is up to the individual to decide which category they should be in. For example, some experts claim that the RSI (Relative Strength Index) represents volatility and momentum, while the MACD (Moving Average Convergence Divergence) is a trend and momentum indicator.

Chapter 2

Trend Indicators

Many seasoned traders will tell you that following the trend is the best way to increase your chances of success. It makes sense to believe that trading with the trend rather than against it would increase your profits.

That's not to argue that countertrend tactics are ineffective. They do, under certain conditions. However, in probability outcomes, it makes sense to recognize the trend and trade in line with it rather than against it.

According to trading lore, markets range 70% of the time and trend just 30% of the time. You can only trend trade thirty percent of the time that markets are open if that assertion is true. Therefore, if you are a trend trader, you must capitalize on a trend occurrence as it arises.

The ADX, or Average Directional Movement Index

The ADX Indicator is a trailing technical indicator for Forex that is developed from the +DI and -DI directional indicators. Its purpose is to display the strength of a trend.

The relationship between the highs, lows, and closing prices of one day and those of the previous day is calculated to determine the Directional Movements, or DIs.

To put it simply, the +DI indicates the strength of the bull relative to yesterday, and the -DI indicates the strength of the bear relative to yesterday. By using the readings of +DI and -DI, the ADX determines whether the bull or the bear is stronger today compared to yesterday.

Use Guide for Adx

ADX is just intended to detect trend strength. Given that it is used appropriately, traders may benefit from the stronger trend indicated by a higher ADX number.

For initiating entry or determining overbought/oversold situations, ADX is not the best tool. Nonetheless, it may provide the trader with information that can indicate if the trend is strong at the moment and, probably more crucially, help determine whether the trader can anticipate the trend to continue.

Using a cut-off number to indicate trends is one popular use of ADX. A trend is seen in readings above the value; stronger trends are indicated by higher values. As a result, a trader may be able to utilize the indicator to indicate the kinds of tactics that should be used.

Trading ADX Indicators

Crossovers

To trade only eligible opportunities in trending markets is the primary goal of employing the ADX. For this reason, it's critical to be aware of +DI and -DI line crossings. It is implied that the rate of positive price movement in the market is higher than the rate of negative price change when the +DI crosses over the –DI line.

When the ADX is over 25, this is a good indication to put purchase orders. Comparably, it indicates that the rate of negative price movement in the market is higher than the rate of positive price change when the -DI crosses over the +DI line. When the ADX falls below 25, this is a strong indication to put sell orders.

Crossovers serve as a catalyst for trade management and exits just as much as they do for trade entrance.

For example, if you are in a long position and the –DI line crosses above +DI, you may use trailing stops to lock in portion of your gains or you can close out of the trade altogether in an attempt to safeguard your cash.

Identifying Ranges

In the markets, the ADX is a reliable range finder. The market is essentially range or trendless when the ADX reading drops below 25 and remains there for a long time. The price of ranging markets bounces off identifiable support and resistance levels. Buy orders are put off support regions and sell orders are placed off resistance areas in these types of markets.

Breakouts

Eventually, a range market will undoubtedly emerge. Market breakouts are common and provide traders with significant opportunities. While it is easy to identify breakouts, it may be quite challenging to assess whether a breakout is legitimate. Too many false breakouts exist that may really trap traders in losing positions. Breakouts are validated in part by the ADX.

That is, it suggests that momentum in the new direction may be maintained when the price breaks out with an ADX value over 25. However, a breakthrough that has an ADX value less than 25 could not hold.

Combining ADX with More Indicators

Due to a few flaws, ADX should not be utilized as a stand-alone indicator. First of all, since it is based on moving averages, it is essentially a lagging indicator that responds to changes in market price more slowly. Additionally, when trading less volatile or range-bound markets, ADX is essentially inefficient. Moreover, ADX crossings might occur often and provide traders with choppy indications. The plan is to use the ADX in conjunction with a supplementary indicator to provide a thorough study of an asset's price. It's crucial to watch out for combining the incorrect signs, since this might result in redundant indicators and information that is overemphasized.

When many indicators are used to assess identical price aspects, it's known as indicator redundancy. For example, the ADX may be used to monitor trend momentum, while stochastic can be used for the same reason. An incorrect mix may also cause one to focus too much on one aspect of the price while ignoring other important indicators.

In the scenario mentioned above, a trader can wind up concentrating on trend momentum and ignoring other crucial factors like volatility.

The following are some of the top ADX indicator combinations that will provide trading signals with a greater probability:

RSI and ADX

When the ADX indicator is less than 25, it indicates that there is no trend in the underlying market. In essence, this is a market that calls for plays with a limited range. RSI provides overbought and oversold trading indications as an oscillator.

When the RSI is over 70, it indicates overbought situations; when it is below 30, it indicates oversold conditions. In a range market, a buy order would be placed if the price is moving down, the ADX reading is less than 25, and the RSI indicates that the market is oversold. Likewise, if the price is beginning to go upward, the RSI is indicating overbought circumstances, and the ADX value is less than 25.

The Parabolic SAR and ADX

When paired with ADX, the leading trend-following Parabolic SAR indicator may assist traders in realizing the most profits possible in a moving market. When three successive parabolas are printed in the direction of a trend, traders may use Parabolic SAR to join a trending market early.

ADX crossovers can take some time to occur in the market. Similarly, when the parabolas flip onto the other side of the trend, Parabolic SAR may provide an early departure signal. Rather of waiting for the +DI and -DI crossings, this may be employed.

Moving Average Convergence/Divergence (MACD)

The purpose of the MACD indicator is to highlight changes in a trend's intensity, course, velocity, and length. The indicator subtracts the 26-period EMA from the 12-period EMA to show the connection between the two exponential moving averages (EMAs).

The indicator often includes:

The outcome of the computation above is the MACD line.

The signal line, or 9-period EMA of the MACD line, is what's utilized to create buy and sell signals.

Diagramming separation between the MACD line and the signal line is called a histogram.

How to Read MACD Average Crossovers

Finding possible trading chances is an excellent approach to read MACD Average Crossovers. Two distinct moving averages are used by the Moving Average Convergence Divergence (MACD) indicator to gauge market momentum. A signal line crossover occurs when the two moving averages cross over one another.

When the shorter-term moving average crosses below the longer-term moving average, this is known as a bearish crossover. This is a negative indication, meaning that momentum is heading south.

Conversely, when the shorter-term moving average crosses above the longer-term moving average, this is known as a bullish crossing. This is a bullish indicator, meaning that the momentum is going upward.

In addition to bullish or bearish divergences, traders may also search for signal line crosses. When the price of the underlying asset is making lower lows and the MACD indicator is rising, this is known as a bullish divergence.

This is a positive indicator, suggesting that a price gain for the asset could be imminent. Conversely, when the price of the underlying asset is rising while the MACD indicator is falling, this is known as a bearish divergence. This is a negative indicator, suggesting that a price decline for the asset could be imminent.

Traders may see possible trading opportunities and decide when to join and quit the market by keeping an eye out for signal line crossings and divergences.

Divergence of MACD

One lagging indicator that may be used to assist find possible buy and sell signals in the forex market is MACD Divergence.

Its foundation is the Moving Average Convergence Divergence (MACD) chart, a technical indicator that contrasts the prices of two moving averages for an asset. Divergence on the MACD chart may indicate an impending buy or sell signal.

When the two moving averages on the MACD chart diverge, it is a buy indication that the security's price is probably going to climb. When the two moving averages on the MACD chart diverge, it is a sell indication that the security's price is probably going to drop. Observing these divergences may help investors make informed decisions about whether to join and quit the market.

Convergence of MACD

When the MACD line and the signal line approach and finally cross over, this is referred to as MACD convergence. Given that the momentum is moving in the other direction, this suggests that the market may be about to reverse its current trend.

When both lines are travelling in the same direction and the MACD line is getting closer to the signal line, convergence has occurred. This suggests that while the momentum is slowing down, the trend is still robust and probably will continue.

Bullish convergence and bearish convergence are the two forms of MACD convergence. When the price keeps falling and the MACD line advances from below to the signal line, this is known as bullish convergence. This suggests that there might be a turnaround to the upside and that the downtrend may be losing steam. Conversely, bearish convergence happens when the price keeps rising as the MACD line moves from above to the signal line. This suggests that there might be a reversal to the negative and that the uptrend may be losing steam.

Limitations with the MACD Indicator

The fact that MACD is a lagging indicator is one of its primary drawbacks. This implies that it may not provide traders with prompt recommendations to act. MACD considers historical price movements rather than present or future ones since it is based on moving averages. Because of this, MACD may not be able to deliver reliable indications in volatile or quickly changing markets.

The possibility of erroneous signals is one more drawback with MACD. When the MACD line crosses the signal line, signaling a shift in trend, MACD creates signals. However, in a sideways or range market, these signals may be deceptive since several crosses may occur without a discernible shift in the direction. Traders should be aware of this and corroborate MACD signals with other indicators or research.

Furthermore, MACD could not perform as well in some asset classes or market circumstances. For instance, some traders could discover that the MACD indicator performs better for equities than for commodities or currencies. The time period being employed may also have an impact on how successful MACD is, since various time frames might provide different signals and outcomes.

Chapter 3

Momentum Indicators

Momentum indicators, often called oscillators, are useful tools for identifying overbought and oversold situations.

They show the speed and size of price changes for a certain security. They may be used in conjunction with trend indicators to assist pinpoint the start and finish of a trend.

Relative Strength Index (RSI)

A widely used momentum indicator that indicates how much relative strength is still in the market move after the motion (momentum) may have peaked is the Relative Strength Index (RSI) indicator.

The RSI computes the relationship between the uptrend and downtrend EMAs while oscillating on a scale of 1 to 100.

It does this by comparing the closing prices of the current and prior candles for the up and down trends. The result is then converted into an EMA (or, in some situations, a SMA). The momentum increases with the size of the gap between today and yesterday.

Therefore, the RSI will be oscillating upward if each closing is higher than the one before it. On the other side, the RSI will be swinging downward if each closing is less than the preceding one. The asset is usually regarded as overbought and may be on the verge of a trend reversal whenever the RSI hits 70. In contrast, a number of 30 indicates an oversold situation for the asset.

Divergence is a familiar idea to the RSI. A bearish signal is produced if the price of the securities makes a higher high but the RSI only produces a lower high, and vice versa.

The Relative Strength Index: Things to Be Aware of

According to conventional wisdom, the Relative Strength Index indicates oversold situations when it is below 30 and overbought conditions when it is over 70. But the levels may be changed to better suit the price movement of a particular investment that a trader is keeping an eye on.

For instance, if a security's RSI often rises above 70 or falls below 30 without accurately indicating a shift in the price trend, a trader may choose to set the upper and/or lower bounds to 80 and 20 respectively to get more dependable trading signals.

Traders should be aware that in times of really strong trends, the price of a security may climb for a considerable amount of time after an oscillator like the RSI flags "overbought" circumstances in the market. The same warning is applicable to price movement in a protracted downturn that could happen long after an RSI signal indicates that the market is "oversold."

Using RSI and other indicators in trading

To improve their comprehension of price movements and their analysis of the market, traders may decide to combine RSI with other indicators. The well-liked indicators listed below could be used in conjunction with an RSI trading strategy.

RSI with Moving Averages (MA)

Moving averages (MA) and relative strength indicator (RSI) are often used by traders to spot trends and possible entry and exit locations.

For instance, a possible long entry may be indicated when the price crosses above a moving average and the RSI leaves the oversold area (above 30). On the other hand, a short entry position may be indicated if the price crosses below the moving average and the RSI rises into overbought zone (over 70).

RSI with Bollinger Bands

An extra confirmation of overbought or oversold circumstances may be obtained by traders by combining Bollinger Bands with RSI.

The asset may be overextended and in need of a correction if the price approaches the upper Bollinger Band and the RSI rises over 70. Similarly, an oversold situation and a buying opportunity may be indicated if the price crosses the lower Bollinger Band and the RSI is below 30.

RSI with MACD

Combining RSI with Moving Average Convergence Divergence (MACD) might provide further evidence of trend and momentum movements. A possible trend reversal to the upside may be strengthened if, for example, RSI exhibits bullish divergence (price makes lower lows while RSI makes higher lows) and MACD crosses above the signal line in a bullish manner.

RSI with Stochastic Oscillator

Similar to RSI, the Stochastic Oscillator indicates overbought and oversold situations. To more accurately assess probable market reversals, traders might compare the two indicators and search for confirmation or divergences. For example, the argument for an upward price movement may be strengthened if the Stochastic Oscillator and RSI both move from overbought to oversold zone.

False signals: Unlike trailing indicators, which may lead you into a good trade later, the RSI is a leading indicator. Leading indicator, on the other hand, are often erroneous signals and are less trustworthy. This is due to the fact that pricing does not always follow changes in momentum.

Size of reversal unknown: Over the years, the RSI indicator has identified several market turning moments, but it is unable to forecast the size of the next price movement. The RSI may be indicating a peak, bottom, or just a brief change in the price trajectory of a company.

By calculating momentum, the Stochastic Oscillator assists in identifying overbought and oversold signs. When it comes to the stochastic, this is accomplished by contrasting a certain closing price with a range of prices across time.

The price should close to the trading range's highs in an uptrend and around its lows in a downtrend. Plotted between a 0 to 100 corridor, the Stochastic is similar to the RSI. Generally speaking, readings below 20 are regarded as oversold, while readings over 80 as overbought.

Chapter 4

Volatility indicators

Volatility indicators show the volume behind the change while identifying ranges. They may be used to forecast future price changes and inform traders about the market's present trend. An entrance signal is often generated by an abrupt shift in market sentiment.

Volatility-based technical indicators for Forex, like all the others discussed before, track changes in market price and compare them to past values.

Average True Range (ATR)

By taking into account the previous closing price as well as the current high and low, the Average True Range Indicator calculates the market's volatility. The biggest of the following is then used to establish the "true range": Current low minus Current high

The new high's absolute value is lower than its prior close.

The new low's absolute value is lower than its prior closure.

Next, the ATR is shown as a moving average of the true ranges for a preset 14-period period. The market's volatility increases when the ATR rises, and vice versa.

The ATR is a helpful tool for determining how much a market may change, but it is not very good for creating trading signals. In turn, this gives you the data you need to decide on important trading choices like position size and where to set your trading limits and stops.

The ATR indicator numbers are easy to understand and interpret. A growing ATR line suggests that the underlying asset's volatility is rising; conversely, a decreasing ATR line suggests that the underlying asset's volatility is falling.

ATR assists traders in monitoring the swings in market volatility, which occur between periods of high and low volatility.

Having a visual representation of volatility might assist traders in establishing firm price goals in the market.

A price objective of less than 100 pip is more likely to be reached during the current trading session, for example, if the GBPJPY has an ATR of 100 pip over the last 14 time periods.

How to Trade using ATR

The ATR is used to calculate the maximum price movement of an asset over a certain period of time. You may utilize this knowledge to trade opportunities like:

Breakouts

When it comes to trading financial assets, breakouts are among the greatest trading chances. The ATR will display low readings to indicate a market with little volatility when prices consolidate.

There is usually a significant degree of volatility during the breakout periods that come after periods of price consolidation. With the aid of the ATR, traders can effectively time these breakouts and take advantage of the chance to enter the new trend at its inception. A spike in the ATR after a stretch of low or flat readings will signal increased market volatility, allowing traders to position themselves for the next breakout.

The Signal Line Method

Since the ATR is merely a volatility measure, it cannot be used to determine the best times to enter a moving market. Traders may fix this by superimposing a moving average, which will serve as a signal line, on the ATR. Traders may, for example, overlay the ATR with a 20-period simple moving average and keep an eye out for crossings. An ATR cross above the signal line indicates a rising trend in prices, and traders may use this confirmation to place aggressive buy orders in the market. Similar to this, if prices are trending down, traders may put aggressive sell orders in the market if the ATR crosses below the signal line, which would confirm a downtrend.

Size of Position

A crucial component of risk management in financial asset trading is position size. Applying the proper lot sizes to various financial assets may greatly improve a trader's ability to limit risk and increase their efficacy in the market. Generally speaking, low volatility markets may be traded with larger lot sizes, whereas high volatility markets should be handled with smaller ones.

Larger lot sizes may be used to trade assets like the EURCHF pair that have lower ATR values, while smaller lot sizes can be used to trade assets like bitcoin and gold that have higher ATR values.

Best ATR Indicator Combinations

Volatility is the sole aspect of price that the ATR monitors. This essentially indicates that in order to find more qualifying trading chances in the market, it is crucial to combine it with other indicators.

The Parabolic SAR and ATR

Trending market trading is best served by using Parabolic SAR. When used in conjunction with the ATR, traders may establish precise stop loss and take-profit levels that guarantee they maximize profits from a moving market while minimizing risk exposure.

ATR and Stochastics

Because they provide alerts for overbought and oversold conditions, stochastics is perfect for trading range markets. In order to prevent whipsaw indications that Stochastics may provide in non-ranging markets, the ATR assists in qualifying ranging markets. Stochastics crosses in overbought and oversold zones may generate buy/sell signals, and low ATR values validate range markets.

Bolinger Band

Another volatility indicator is Bollinger Bands, which are made up of three bands: a SMA (with a default value of

20) encircled by two extra trendlines that are computed as follows:

SMA less two standard deviations equal the lower band.

SMA + two standard deviations equal the upper band.

As a consequence, the price of the security might move about in a dynamic corridor. The trader has the ability to modify all of the settings to suit their tastes.

The market is deemed overbought when prices are close to the upper deviation line and oversold when they are near the lower deviation line. Moreover, the Bollinger Bands will expand in a market that is more volatile and shrink in a market that is less volatile.

Using Bollinger Bands to Trade

Many traders utilize Bollinger Bands, a well-liked trading technique tool, to find possible buy and sell signals.

The technique uses volatility bands above and below the price chart to identify overbought and oversold conditions on an asset.

When using Bollinger Bands to purchase low, watch for moments when an asset's price dips towards the lower band.

This suggests that the asset may have been oversold, which means it's worth may be underestimated and a price reversal is likely.

After spotting this indication, think about buying the asset at the market price.

When using Bollinger Bands to sell high, watch for situations when prices go up near or above the upper band.

This implies that an asset could be overpriced and might see a rapid decline in value.

In this case, it may be prudent to sell off a portion of your assets at current market prices prior to a large collapse.

It's important to remember that, despite their potential use as trading tools, these signals are not necessarily reliable predictors of future market moves.

Bollinger Bands should thus be used in conjunction with other analytical techniques to ensure a full assessment of investing choices.

Advantages And the Disadvantages of Bollinger Bands Techniques

Bollinger Bands are an important indicator, as shown by what we have mentioned so far, but they also have drawbacks.

To begin with the advantages:

They provide you with a graphic depiction of volatility, which facilitates evaluating the state of the market;

They may be used to establish and implement various strategies; They are very popular: adopting popular indicators is crucial when it comes to investing, particularly in the forex market, as it indicates that a large number of traders globally are making the same decisions, which drives prices in certain directions;

Because of their widespread use, it's very easy to locate trading platforms that use this indicator;

Bollinger Bands are strong despite having a simple construction;

They may be used in many periods;

These may be used to examine volatility and potential new trend initiation.

The main disadvantage of this indicator is that you have to be able to configure the bands in accordance with the particular market you are investing in. Technical analysis is really more of an art than a science as it requires you to examine an asset's behavior and determine if the most often used parameters are feasible. If not, you would have to make decisions like changing the simple moving average's length to better suit the specific requirements of the market.

Bollinger Bands are a useful instrument since they belong to the class of oscillators, which are specialized technical indicators that use ranges rather than set price points.

This increases your trading strategy options and potential earnings, but it also necessitates the ability to choose the right parameters.

Furthermore, you cannot attempt to make longer-term forecasts using these bands; instead, they are more useful for assessing the present or very short-term market circumstances.

Chapter 5

Volume Indicators

The volume of transactions underlying a price change is shown via volume indicators. More traders entering the market must be doing so for group motivations. Are they responding to a breaking news story or the publication of the economic calendar.

Unlike, say, equities, commodities, or even Forex futures, it is difficult to measure the whole market volume of the Forex spot market at the pace and depth necessary by traders. This is due to the fact that Forex spot is dealt over-the-counter (OTC), meaning there isn't a single clearinghouse where volumes can be recalculated.

The volume that is accessible on your platform is sourced from the data stream owned by your broker. Those figures are by no means representative of the whole global volume. That being said, some traders use volume indicators in their Forex trading, and some of them may even be profitable.

On-Balance Volume (OBV)

The OBV Indicator is used to calculate changes in an instrument's volume in relation to its price. This is in line with the theory that volume may be used to corroborate price movements since it changes before price.

If the total daily volume rises from the day before, it is given a positive value. Likewise, if the overall volume is lower than it was the day before, a negative value is given. The OBV should rise sharply in tandem with a strong trend in pricing. A difference between the price and the OBV would suggest that the market move was less than expected.

On-Balance Volume is One of the first trading indicators in the financial markets, which was created in 1963 by stock market forecaster Joseph Granville. OBV forecasts and indicates changes in stock or asset prices based on the flow of money, or volume. OBV, to put it simply, is a price-to-volume comparison of an asset.

The current trade volume is added to or subtracted from the prior OBV number in order to compute OBV. When the price of bitcoin closes higher than it did the day before, the prior OBV and trading volume must be included. If, however, the market price ends at a lower level than it did the day before, you deduct the trading volume.

OBV is a momentum indicator that lets you determine price trends for any asset by looking at variations in volume. It gives you information about investor sentiment, enabling you to predict trends that will rise or fall. In addition, compared to volume histograms, it provides more meaningful indicators.

Money Flow Index (MFI)
One of the greatest measures for assessing trade pressure in the FX market is the Money Flow Index (MFI). When

analyzing purchasing or selling pressure in the market, the MFI takes time and price into account.

Relative Strength Index (RSI) and MFI indicator operation is comparable, with volume being the primary distinction. This indicator, sometimes known as volume-weighted RSI, may occasionally provide light on variations in volume.

In essence, the MFI is a line with values between 0 and 100, where larger numbers indicate more purchasing demand. There may have been overbuying in the market if the indicator climbs near the 80–90 level. In a similar vein, overselling of an asset may be indicated when the MFI line approaches 10 or 20.

How to Trade with the MFI Indicator

The MFI indicator is often included with popular trading systems like Trading View, MT4, and MT5. On MT4 and

MT5, click "Indicators" on the top left menu and go to the volumes folder to find it.

Next, you will locate the MFI indicator. After selecting the "Indicators" option at the top of your current chart in Trading View, you can quickly search for and find the indicator. You will be able to see the indicator as a sub-chart underneath the main chart after you have added it successfully.

The indicator chart appears as a line graph with oscillations between 0 and 100 values. Although some traders like to utilize greater periods to obtain more precise trading signals, the default period is 14. Like many other indicators, the indicator generally gives fewer trade signals but with much greater accuracy the higher the period, as it gathers more price data.

Lastly, a band extending from the 20 level to the 100 level, with the 50-level serving as a symbol of market equilibrium, is also included in the indicator in its default condition. The trading approach of the indicator relies heavily on these levels.

After setting up your indicator, you may trade it in the following ways:

Oversold and Overbought Regions

When the MFI indicator reaches the 20 and 80 marks, you may trade on it. You know the instrument is oversold and are ready to purchase when the index drops below 20.

Try not to purchase, however, until the indicator goes back within the 20–80 band. On the other hand, if the index rises over 80, the instrument is overbought and you should prepare to sell.

The indication to sell is when the indicator moves back into the 20–80 area. And that was the MFI trading approach in the beginning.

Divergence

Trading the divergences between the indicator and price movement is another method of using the MFI indicator. The index or indicator often follows the fluctuation of the price. However, there is a divergence when the price seems to have moved against the index. Additionally, it often signals the impending reversal in price.

Trend Trading

Apart from the divergence and overbought/oversold trading techniques, there exists an additional method of using the Money Flow Index indicator in conjunction with the Moving Average indicator. Usually, this method is used to identify trends and trade them using the trend trading approach.

The MFI and the MA are first opened in the same window. Open your MFI in Trading View first in order to do this. "MFI 14" is located in the upper left corner of the indicator pane. Touch and hold it to reveal more buttons. Hover your cursor over each of these new choices, then click "More." Lastly, choose "Add indicator to MFI 14" from the choice that displays. Find and choose your Moving Average (MA) indicator, then set its period to thirty.

The Money Flow Index Indicator's Advantages

When used properly, the Money Flow Indicator is a fantastic trading tool with a high success rate. It is regarded as an accurate indicator and is rather simple to use, particularly for short-term traders.

Compared to other indicators in its class, the MFI indicator calls trade signals more quickly since it integrates price and volume data.

Additionally, the volume data's inclusion provides a more trustworthy understanding of the prevailing market circumstances.

Because the MFI indicator is so easy to use and implement, customers may devote more effort to its profitability rather than its feasibility.

It provides trading indications in a variety of formats, including divergence circumstances, the onset of new trends, and overbought and oversold situations.

Limitations with the MFI indicator

The Money Flow Index has several advantages, but it also has certain drawbacks. It is recommended to employ additional indicators to validate the indications given by the MFI indicator since, in the first place, it could offer erroneous signals.

Furthermore, because of its parameters based on price and volume data, it may remain in overbought or oversold zones for an extended period of time, which might cause traders to lose out on profitable trading chances.

The MFI indicator has a tendency to provide false positives. It's possible that price activity will not follow the recommended indication.

Additionally, the indicator may not call signals when it ought to, which might lead to the loss of a potentially successful trading position.